T. E. Lawrence:

A Bibliography

T. E. Lawrence:
A
Bibliography

Jeffrey Meyers

Garland Publishing, Inc., New York & London

Library of Congress Cataloging in Publication Data

Meyers, Jeffrey.
    T. E. Lawrence: a bibliography.

    1. Lawrence, Thomas Edward, 1888-1935--Bibliography.
I. Title.
Z8491.5.M48   016.828'9'1208   74-11361
ISBN 0-8240-1052-3

For Joyce

Preface

In Part I of this bibliography I have omitted the various editions and translations of Lawrence's works and all the essays later included in *Evolution of a Revolt*. In Part II I have omitted the ephemera, almost all newspaper articles, most book reviews, foreign editions of books translated into English, and books that merely refer to Lawrence. Despite this selectivity, the majority of the works included here are of poor quality and I have used the following symbols to make some discriminations: * for the more significant works, Rev for book reviews, R for reprints, F for essays included in *T.E. Lawrence By His Friends*, and B for boys' books. The bibliographies by Frank Baxter, Theodora Duncan, Elizabeth Duval and Guyla Houston have been very useful.

I. WORKS OF T.E. LAWRENCE:

A. Books:

Cancelled First Chapter of Seven Pillars of Wisdom with Sixteen Letters by
      Lawrence and a Memoir by Ralph Isham, New York, 1937

Colonel Lawrence of Arabia: His Original Manuscript Autobiography and
      Correspondence with Robert Graves, London: Maggs Bros., 1936

Crusader Castles, 2 vols, London, 1936

The Diary of T.E. Lawrence, MCMXI, London, 1937

Eight Letters From T.E. Lawrence, ed. Harley Granville-Barker, London,
      1939

An Essay on Flecker, London, 1937

The Essential T.E. Lawrence, ed. David Garnett, London, 1951

The Evolution of a Revolt: Early Postwar Writings of T.E. Lawrence, eds.
      and intro. Stanley and Rodelle Weintraub, University Park, Pa., 1968

      /J.H. Ross, trans./, The Forest Giant by Adrian LeCorbeau, London,
      1935

      'A Handbook to the $37\frac{1}{2}$ Foot Motor Boats of the 200 Class', 1933.
      /Typewritten, in the Houghton Library/

The Home Letters of T.E. Lawrence and His Brothers, Intro. by Winston
      Churchill, Oxford, 1954

A Letter from T.E. Lawrence to His Mother, London: Corvinus, 1936

Letters from T.E. Shaw to Viscount Carlow, London: Corvinus, 1936

The Letters of T.E. Lawrence, ed. and intro. David Garnett
      Foreword by B.H. Liddell Hart, London, 1964

Letters from T.E. Shaw to Bruce Rogers, New Fairfield, Conn., 1933

      /T.E. Shaw/, Letters to H.S. Ede, 1927-1935, London, 1942.

Men in Print: Essays in Literary Criticism, Intro. by A.W. Lawrence, London, 1940

Minorities, ed. J.M. Wilson, Preface by C. Day Lewis, London, 1971

The Mint, Intro. by A.W. Lawrence, London, 1955

More Letters from T.E. Shaw to Bruce Rogers, New Fairfield, Conn., 1936

　　/T.E. Shaw, trans./, The Odyssey of Homer, Intro. by John Finley, New York, 1932

Oriental Assembly, ed. A.W. Lawrence, London, 1939

Revolt in the Desert, New York, 1927

Secret Despatches from Arabia, Foreword by A.W. Lawrence, London, 1939

Seven Pillars of Wisdom, Bibliographical note /holograph/ by Edward Garnett, Oxford, 1922, Houghton Library

Seven Pillars of Wisdom, /London/, 1926

Seven Pillars of Wisdom, New York, 1935

Selections from Seven Pillars of Wisdom, ed. John Cullen, London, 1961

T.E. Lawrence to His Biographers Robert Graves and Liddell-Hart, London, 1963

　　/trans./, Two Arabic Tales, London, 1937

　　/and Philip Graves, eds./, Great Britain, War Office, Intelligence Division, Handbook of the Turkish Army, Cairo, 1915

　　/and D.G. Hogarth, eds./, The Arab Bulletin, Cairo, 6 June 1916-6 December 1918.

　　and C. Leonard Woolley, Carchemish: Report on the Excavations at Djerabis on Behalf of the British Museum, London, 1914

　　and C. Leonard Woolley, 'The Wilderness of Zin', Palestine Exploration Fund Annual, London, 1915

B. Essays:

R 'Adventure in Arabia', <u>Great True Adventures</u>, ed. Lowell Thomas, New York, 1955. Pp. 93-111

R 'All Out of Aristophanes or Juvenal', <u>Letters to Mother: An Anthology</u>, ed. Charles Van Doren, New York, 1959. Pp. 65-9

'Among the Bedouins', <u>Empire News</u>, 9 June 1935, p. 7

'Arabian Politics', <u>Morning Post</u> ∕London∕, 20 July 1922, p. 8

R 'Blowing Up A Train', <u>With Fire and Sword</u>, eds. Quentin Reynolds and Robert Leckie, New York, 1963. Pp. 199-208

'Campaign of the Caliphs for Damascus', <u>Current History</u>, IX (February 1919), 348-57

R 'Cartas de T.E. Lawrence a Lionel Curtis', <u>Sur</u>, C (enero 1943), 7-22

'The Changing East', <u>Round Table</u>, X (September 1920), 756-72

R 'The Conquest of Damascus', <u>World's Work</u>, LIV (May 1927), 36-53

∕C.D. (Colin Dale)∕, 'A Critic of Critics Criticised', <u>Spectator</u>, CXXXIX (27 August 1927), 321-22

∕C.D.∕, 'D.H. Lawrence's Novels', <u>Spectator</u>, CXXXIX (6 August 1927), 223

R 'Dynamiting Turks', <u>World's Work</u>, LIII (March 1927), 513-33

R 'Extracts from Lawrence's <u>Twenty-Seven Articles</u>', <u>Military Review</u>, XXXIV (October 1954), 28-30

R 'The Fear', <u>New Republic</u>, CXXXII (21 March 1955), 18-19

'Ferment for Freedom: Colonel Lawrence on the Eastern Problem', <u>Daily Herald</u> ∕London∕, 9 August 1920, p. 2

R 'Fomenting Revolt in Arabia', <u>World's Work</u>, LIII (February 1927), 369-92

R 'Guerrilla: Science of Guerrilla Warfare', <u>Encyclopedia Britannica</u>, X (London, 1948), 950-3

∕C.D.∕, 'Hakluyt - First Naval Propagandist', <u>Spectator</u>, CXXXIX (10 September 1927), 390-1

'Introduction' to Travels in Arabia Deserta by Charles Doughty, London, 1921. Pp. xvii–xxvii

R 'Arabia Deserta: Vorwort zu dem Arabien-Buch von Charles Doughty', trans. Hertha Federman, Neue Rundschau, XLVIII (July 1937), 88–102

'Introduction' to Arabia Felix: Across the Empty Quarter of Arabia by Bertram Thomas, London, 1932. Pp. xvii–xx

R 'Arabian Travellers', Then and Now, London, 1935. Pp. 93–6

'Introduction' to Twilight of the Gods by Richard Garnett, New York, 1926. Pp. vii–xiv

/C.J.G./, 'The Kaer of Ibu Wardani', Jesus College Magazine, I (January 1913), 37–9

/trans./, 'Lawrence's Note in Facsimile', Times /London/, 10 June 1936, p. 15

'Letter' (27 February 1925). Post-Bag Diversions. ed. E.V. Lucas. London, 1934. p. 183

R 'Letter to Robert Graves', World Review, VIII (October 1949), 66

R 'Letters of T.E. Lawrence', ed. David Garnett, Atlantic Monthly, CLXIII (February–March 1939), 147–57, 327–37

R 'Letters to Lionel Curtis', A Second Treasury of the World's Great Letters, eds. Wallace Brockway and Bart Winer, London, 1950. Pp. 535–40

R 'Une lettre de T.E. Lawrence', Le Maison sans issues par James Hanley, Intro. by Henry Miller, Londres-Bruxelles, s.d. Pp. 11–13

R 'Lettres 1910–1935', Les temps modernes, XXXII–XXXV (mai, juin, août 1948), 1944–75, 2177–98, 265–89

'Massacre', The Winter Owl, eds. Robert Graves and William Nicholson, III (1923), 5–13

R 'Massacre', Living Age, 321 (3 May 1924), 858–64

/C.D./, 'Mixed Biscuits', Spectator, CXXXIX (20 August 1927), 290–1

'Myself', Evening Standard /London/, 20 May 1935. pp. 1, 4

'Notes Dictated to E.H.T. Robinson during the Arabian Campaign.' /Typewritten, in the Imperial War Museum/

'Preface' to Leicester Galleries, Catalogue of an Exhibition of Paintings, Pastels, Drawings and Woodcuts Illustrating Colonel T.E. Lawrence's 'Seven Pillars of Wisdom'. Another Preface by G.B. Shaw, London, 1927

'Prefatory Letter' to The Imperial Camel Corps with Colonel Lawrence by Capt. Douglas Pearman, London, 1928

'Prefatory Letter' to River Niger by Simon Jesty, London, 1935. Pp. 11-13

R 'A Raid in the Desert', The Essay, ed. John Stewart, New York, 1952. Pp. 463-72

/T.E. Shaw/, 'Ramping', Journal of the R.A.F. College, Cranwell, XV (Autumn 1935), 152-3

/'Report from Damascus'/, Allenby's Final Triumph by William Massey, London, 1920. Pp. 342-3

'The Revolt in the Desert', Daily Telegraph /London/, 15 December 1926-10 January 1927

R 'Revolt in the Desert', Armageddon: The World War in Literature, ed. Eugene Löhrke, New York, 1930. Pp. 348-63

R 'The Road', Man and Motor: The Twentieth Century Love Affair, ed. Derek Jewell, London, 1966. Pp. 133-5

'Service Life', British Legion Journal, XIII (November 1933), 160-1, 169

'A Set Piece: January 1918', Army Quarterly, II (April 1921), 22-31

/T.E. Shaw/, Some Notes on the Writing of Seven Pillars of Wisdom, London, 1926

R 'A Spouting Column of Dust and Smoke', The Book of the Earth, ed. August Spectorsky, New York, 1957. Pp. 383-9

R 'Torture' and 'Blowing Up A Train', Men at War, ed. and intro. Ernest Hemingway, New York, 1942. Pp. 303-8, 522-8

'Translation of an Arabic Poem by the Emir Feisal', The Saturday Book, ed. Leonard Russell, London, 1951. P. 175

'Two Unpublished Letters', Nine, II (Summer 1950), 180-2

'An Unpublished Letter of Lawrence of Arabia', National Review, XV (10 September 1963), 203-5

R The Voyages of Ulysses: A Photographic Interpretation of Homer's Odyssey by Erich Lessing with Selections from T.E. Lawrence's Translation, London, 1966

'War in the Desert'. An Anthology of Modern Travel Writing. ed. H.M. Tomlinson. London, 1936. Pp. 96-100

'The Wells Short Stories', Spectator, CXL (25 February 1928), 268-9

R 'With Lawrence's Guerrillas: How They Helped Allenby in a Holy War', World's Work, LIII (April 1927), 643-63

II. WORKS ON T.E. LAWRENCE:

Abdullah, Memoirs of King Abdullah of Transjordan, ed. Philip Graves, Intro. R.J.C. Broadhurst, London, 1950

Adam, Colin, The Life of Lord Lloyd, London, 1948. Pp. 199-200, 211-12, 262-4

Adam, Paul, Les Echecs de T.E. Lawrence. n.p., n.d. (privately printed).

Adam, Ruth, What Shaw Really Said, New York, 1966, pp. 82-4, 167

Adams, James, 'Ordeal in Arabia', Triumph Over Odds, New York, 1957. Pp. 383-89

Addison, William, Epping Forest - Its Literary and Historical Associations, London, 1946. Pp. 224-5

Akdemir, Aziz Hudin, Turk Duşmani Casus Lavrens ve Benzerleri, /The Agent Lawrence, Enemy of Turkey, and Similar Ones7, Istanbul, 1950

Aldanov, A., 'Le roi Feyçal et le colonel Lawrence', Revue de France, XV (1935), 622-46

*Aldington, Richard, Lawrence of Arabia: A Biographical Enquiry, London, 1955

Aldridge, James, Heroes of the Empty View, London, 1954

Allen, H. Warner, 'The Tragedy of Lawrence', Saturday Review, CLX (7 September 1935), 143

R Allenby, Gen. Edmund, 'Colonel T.E. Lawrence', Journal of the Central Asian Society, XXII (July 1935), 333

F ——. 'Lord Allenby's Tribute', The Times /London7, 20 May 1935, p. 16

R, F ——, and Sir Herbert Baker, 'Tributes to Lawrence of Arabia: In War; In Peace', Listener, XIII (22 May 1935), 857-8

Altounyan, Ernest, Ornament of Honour, Cambridge, England, 1937

Rev Alvarez, A., 'Arabia Deserta', New Statesman, LIX (21 May 1960), 748, 750

Rev ——, 'Testimonials', New Statesman, LXIV (3 August 1962), 150-1

American Art Association, Anderson Galleries, Catalogue no. 4320, New York, 15 April 1937. Pp. 109-24

Antonius, George, The Arab Awakening, London, 1938

Arendt, Hannah, 'The Imperialist Character', Review of Politics, XII (July 1950), 316-20

R ——, The Origins of Totalitarianism, New York, 1951. Pp. 218-21

Armbrister, Trevor, 'O'Toole of Arabia', Saturday Evening Post, CCXXXVI (9 March 1963), 22-8

*Armitage, Flora, The Desert and the Stars, New York, 1955

——, 'The Home of Lawrence of Arabia', Contemporary Review, CLXXXIII (January 1953), 35-9

Arnand, R., 'Lawrence l'Arabe; ou la guerre au désert', Annales politiques et littéraires, CV (25 juin 1935), 632-5

Arnold, Julian, Lawrence of Arabia, Los Angeles, 1935. /Pamphlet/

——, 'T.E. Lawrence', Giants in Dressing Gowns, Chicago, 1942. Pp. 140-4

——, 'Lawrence MS Bought by Wells', Art News, XXXIV (26 October 1935), 4

Auden, W.H., 'A Happy New Year', New Country, ed. Michael Roberts, London, 1933. P. 199

——, 'T.E. Lawrence', Then and Now, London, 1935. Pp. 21-3

—— and Christopher Isherwood, The Ascent of F-6, New York, 1937

Rev B., 'Crusader Castles', Palestine Exploration Fund. Quarterly Statement, LXVIII-LXIX (October 1936, January 1937), 231-4, 79-81

Baker, Sir Herbert, Architecture and Personalities, London, 1944. Pp. 195-8, 206

Banse, Ewald, Lawrence, der ungeberönte König der Araber, Dresden, 1937

Barber, D.F., ed. Concerning Thomas Hardy, London, 1968. Pp. 112, 118, 142-3, 157

B Barbery, James, Lawrence and His Desert Raiders, London, 1965

Barker, A.R.V., 'An Epic of the Desert War', World Today, XLIX (April 1927), 445-50

Barker, Sir Ernest. Age and Youth: Memories of Three Universities. London, 1953. Pp. 60-61

Barnett, R.D., 'T.E. Lawrence and the British Museum', TLS, 16 October 1969, pp. 1210-11

Barrow, General George, The Fire of Life, London, 1942. Pp. 204-15

*Baxter, Frank, An Annotated Check-List of a Collection of Writings By and About T.E. Lawrence, Los Angeles, 1968

———, 'Some Notes on Lawrence of Arabia', Coranto, I (Spring 1964), 24-30

Bell, Gertrude, The Letters of Gertrude Bell, London, 1927. 2 vols

Bellis, Hannah, 'T.E. Lawrence', They Made History, London, 1963. IV, 45-64

Bennett, Alan, Forty Years On, London, 1969. Pp. 38-40, 75

Benoist-Méchin, Jacques, Arabian Destiny, Fair Lawn, New Jersey, 1958. Pp. 150-3, 157-8, 170-3

———, Lawrence d'Arabie, ou le rêve fracassé, Lausanne, 1961

Bentwich, Norman, My 77 Years, Philadelphia, 1961. Pp. 33-4, 42, 69-70

Bernard, Henri, 'Presence de Lawrence', Guerre totale et guerre révolutionnaire, Bruxelles, 1965, I, 411-25

Rev Bidwell, Shelford, 'A Military View of T.E. Lawrence', Army Quarterly, C (1970), 71-3

Rev Bielstein, Hans, 'Wassmuss und Lawrence: Ein Vergleich', Westermanns Monatshefte, CLXVIII (March 1940), 383

Birdwood, Christopher Lord, Nuri as-Said: A Study in Arab Leadership, London, 1959. Pp. 41-88, 102-27

Bishop, Edward, The Debt We Owe: The Royal Air Force Benevolent Fund, London, 1969. Pp. 14-18, 121

*Blackmur, R.P., 'The Everlasting Effort: A Citation of T.E. Lawrence', The Expense of Greatness, New York, 1940. Pp. 1-36

R ——, 'The Everlasting Effort: A Citation of T.E. Lawrence', The Lion and the Honeycomb, New York, 1955. Pp. 97-123

Blanc-Dufour, A., 'L'Agent double', Cahiers du Sud, XXVIII (1948), 546-9

Blankfort, Michael, Behold the Fire, New York, 1965

Blumenfeld, R.D., All in a Lifetime. London, 1931. P. 136

——, 'The Mechanised Prince of Mecca'. R.D.B.'s Procession. London, 1935. Pp. 115-117

Blunt, Wilfred, Cockerell: A Life of Sir Sydney Cockerell, London, 1964

*Blythe, Ronald, 'Sublimated Aladdin', The Age of Illusion: England in the Twenties and Thirties, London, 1963. Pp. 63-82

Boak, Denis, André Malraux, Oxford, 1968. Pp. 3-5, 147-8, 209-11

* ——, 'Malraux and T.E. Lawrence', Modern Language Review, LXI (1966), 218-224

Boisdeffre, Pierre de, 'Le Colonel Lawrence ou la tentation du Néant', Etudes, 287 (novembre 1955), 168-82

——, 'T.E. Lawrence, héritier de Nietzsche', Journal de Genève (24-5 février 1952), pp. 3-4

R Bolitho, Hector, The Angry Neighbours, London, 1957. Pp. 137-9

——, Older People, New York, 1935. Pp. 257-60

——, 'T.E. Lawrence and Lord Alfred Douglas: Reminiscences', Theatre World, LVI (September 1960), 30-1

Bolt, Robert, 'Clues to the Legend of Lawrence', New York Times Magazine, 25 February 1962, pp. 16-17, 45, 48, 50

——, 'Lawrence Meets Feisal', Show, II (December 1962), 68-9, 132

——, 'Lawrence of Arabia' /screenplay/, 1962

——, 'The Playwright in Films', Saturday Review, XLV (29 December 1962), 15-16. See also 29-30

B Bond, Geoffrey, The Lawrence of Arabia Story, London, 1960

*Bonsal, Stephen, 'Arabs Plead for Freedom', Suitors and Supplicants: The Little Nations at Versailles, New York, 1946. Pp. 32-51

——, 'Lawrence - Speaks From the Grave', Los Angeles Times Sunday Magazine. 12 January 1936, pp. 7-8

B Bourgeois, Willy, Lawrence, roi secret de l'Arabie, Verviers, Belgique, 1957

Boussard, Léon, Le secret du colonel Lawrence, Paris, 1946

Bowden, Ann, 'The T.E. Lawrence Collection at the University of Texas', Texas Quarterly, V (1962), 54-63

Bowen, Elizabeth, 'Lawrence of Arabia', Show, II (December 1962), 66-7

Rev Bowers, Fredson, 'Letters of a Man of Legend', Virginia Quarterly Review, XV (Summer 1939), 479-80

Bowman, Humphrey, Middle-East Window, London, 1942. Pp. 180-1

Bowra, Sir Maurice, 'Introduction' to T.E. Shaw's translation of the Odyssey, London: O.U.P., 1955. Pp. vii-xvi

Boxhall, P.G., 'Two Studies in Destiny; Being an Investigation into the Comparative Characteristics of T.E. Lawrence and Orde Wingate', Army Quarterly and Defence Journal, LXXXIX (January 1965), 206-11

Boyle, Andrew, Montagu Norman, London, 1967. Pp. 296-7

——, Trenchard, London, 1962

/Boyle, W.H.D./ Earl of Cork and Orrery, My Naval Life, 1886-1941, London, 1942. Pp. 99-104

Bray, Major Norman, Shifting Sands, London, 1934

Braybrooke, Neville, 'Vocation in the Desert: Lawrence of Arabia and Charles de Foucauld', Commonweal, XCIV (2 April 1971), 88-9

Brémond, Edouard, Le Hedjaz dans la Guerre Mondiale, Paris, 1931

Rev Brennecke, Ernest, Jr., 'English Arabs', Commonweal, XVII (8 February 1933), 406-8

B Bridges, Thomas and Tiltman, Hubert, 'Lawrence of Arabia', Heroes of Modern Adventure, New York, 1927. Pp. 174-93

Rev Brion, M., 'Les Sept Piliers de la Sagesse par T.E. Lawrence', Cahiers du Sud, XVII (mai 1938), 400-4

'Lawrence of Arabia at Clouds Hill', BBC broadcast, 3 December 1958

'T.E. Lawrence: 1888-1935', BBC broadcast, 27 November 1962

Brodie, I.E., 'Lawrence Was My Orderly', NAAFI Review (Summer 1963), 6-7

Brodrick, Alan, 'With Lawrence in Arabia', Near to Greatness: A Life of the Sixth Earl Winterton, London, 1965. Pp. 177-85

Bromage, Bernard, 'Difficulty of the Way: An Essay on T.E. Lawrence', Occult Review, LXIV (October 1937), 255-61

Brooks, Cleanth and Warren, Robert Penn, Modern Rhetoric, New York, 1961. Pp. 175, 181, 299-300, 305-8

Brophy, John, Flesh and Blood, London, 1931

Broughton, Harry, Lawrence of Arabia and Dorset, Wareham, England, 1966

——, Lawrence of Arabia and Wareham, Wareham, England, 1965

——, Lawrence of Arabia: The Facts Without the Fiction, Wareham, England, 1969

Brown, Oliver, Exhibition: Memoirs, London, 1968. Pp. 77-8, 99-100, 107, 176-9, 181-4

Brownrigg, Lt.-General Sir Douglas, Unexpected: A Book of Memories, London, n.d. Pp. 58-9

Bruce, John, 'I Knew Lawrence', Scottish Field (August 1938), pp. 20-1

Buchan, John, Courts of the Morning, London, 1929

——, Greenmantle, London, 1916

F ——, Memory Hold the Door, London, 1940. Pp. 211-18.
    /American edition called Pilgrim's Way/

Rev ——, 'Of Such Is History', Saturday Review of Literature, III (19 March 1927), 659-60

Rev, R ——, 'Revolt in the Desert by T.E. Lawrence', Designed for Reading: An Anthology From the Saturday Review of Literature, New York, 1934. Pp. 316-20

——, /Lord Tweedsmuir/, 'T.E. Lawrence', Canadian Defence Quarterly, XVI (July 1939), 371-8

/Buchan, Susan/, John Buchan By His Wife and Friends, London, 1947. Pp. 162, 192-5, 230

'T.E. Lawrence: An Effigy in Wareham Church, Dorset', Builder, CLVIII (22 March 1940), 354, 359

Bullard, Sir Reader, The Camels Must Go, London, 1961. Pp. 121-2, 158-9

Burbidge, William, The Mysterious AC2: A Biographical Sketch of Lawrence of Arabia, London, 1943

Burford, William, 'Lawrence/Ross/Shaw', Texas Quarterly, V (1962), 33

Burgoyne, Elizabeth, Gertrude Bell, 1914-1926, London, 1961. Pp. 108-10, 162-5

Burton, Percy and Thomas, Lowell, 'From Sherlock Holmes to T.E. Lawrence', Adventures Among Immortals, New York, 1937. Pp. 272-9

Busch, Briton, Britain, India and the Arabs, 1914-1921, Berkeley, 1971

Butler, J.R.M., Lord Lothian (Philip Kerr) 1882-1940, London, 1960. Pp. 245-6

Rev Butler, P.R., 'T.E. Lawrence', Quarterly Review, CCLXVI (April 1936), 219-34

B Cadell, James /pseud. of Ronald Thomas/, Young Lawrence of Arabia, London, 1962

Cadiz-Avila, I., 'Lawrenciana: Recuerdos de Lawrence de Arabia', El Mercurio /Santiago, Chile/, 20 March 1966

Rev Caillois, Roland, 'L'Echec de T.E. Lawrence', Critique, IV (février 1948), 100-7

Campbell, Olwen, 'Some Reflections on the Life of T.E. Lawrence', The Lighted Window, Cambridge, England, 1940. Pp. 9-36

Rev Canby, Henry, 'The Last Great Puritan', Saturday Review, XII (September 1935), 3-4, 14

Rev, R ——. 'The Last Great Puritan', Seven Years Harvest, New York, 1936. Pp. 40-6

Rev ——, 'Lawrence After Arabia', Saturday Review, XV (21 November 1936), 5-7

Candler, Edmund, 'Lawrence and the Hejaz', Blackwood's, CCXVIII (December 1925), 733-61

R ——. 'Lawrence and the Hejaz', Atlantic Monthly, CXXXVII (March 1926), 289-304

Rev Carrington, C.E., 'T.E. Lawrence', Contemporary Review, CCXV (December 1969), 281-7

Castro e Almeida, Virgínia de, Lawrence e os Arabes, Lisboa, 1943

Caudwell, Christopher, 'T.E. Lawrence: A Study in Heroism', Studies in a Dying Culture. London, 1938. Pp. 20-43

Chappelow, Alan, ed., Shaw the Villager and Human Being, New York, 1962. Pp. 53, 123-4, 162-3

Chew, Samuel, 'Anthropology; Travel; History; Criticism', A Literary History of England, ed. Albert Baugh, New York, 1948. Pp. 1592-4

   'Lawrence of Arabia: War's Spiritual Toll', Christian Century, LII (29 May 1935), 717-18

R Churchill, Winston, 'Lawrence of Arabia', Ex-Services of Malaya Magazine (Autumn 1935), pp. 19-20, 22-4

F ——, 'Lawrence of Arabia', Great Contemporaries, London, 1937. Pp. 129-40

Rev ——, 'Lawrence's Great Book', Daily Mail /London/, 29 July 1935, p. 8

Clark, Ronald, Brough Superior: the Rolls-Royce of Motor Cycles. Norwich, 1964. Pp. 117-25, 141

Clements, Frank, T.E. Lawrence: A Reader's Guide. Newton Abbot, 1972

Cobern, Camden, 'Preface', Recent Explorations in Palestine, 3rd edition, Meadville, Penna, 1916. Pp. 5-13

Cohen, Gustav, 'Affaire Aldington contre Lawrence d'Arabie', Hommes et mondes, CXVI (mars 1956), 487-96

B Collier, Douglas, 'Thomas Edward Lawrence', 100 Great Modern Lives, ed. John Canning, London, 1965. Pp. 516-20

Collis, Maurice, Nancy Astor: An Informal Biography, New York, 1960.
Pp. 150-3, 217

Columbia Pictures, Lawrence of Arabia, New York, 1962

Connell, John, Wavell: Soldier and Scholar, London, 1964. Pp. 175-6

Cook, Albert, 'T.E. Lawrence', The Meaning of Fiction, Detroit, 1960.
Pp. 273-9

Corbett, Capt. H.A., 'A Critic in Action', Royal United Service Institute
Journal, CVIII (November 1963), 366-70

Cosyns-Verhaegen, Roger, T.E. Lawrence: l'apprenti-sorcier de la guerre
subversive, Bruxelles, 1961

Coward, Nöel, Future Indefinite, New York, 1954. Pp. 263-5

Rev Cowley, Malcolm, 'The Road to Damascus', New Republic, LXXXIV
(9 October 1935), 248-9

Cross, L.B., 'Lawrence of Arabia', Modern Churchman, XXV (July 1935),
236-42

Cumming, Henry, Franco-British Rivalry in the Post-War Near East, New
York, 1938

Cunliffe, John, 'Essays, Journalism and Travel: T.E. Lawrence', English
Literature in the Twentieth Century, New York, 1933. Pp. 275-80

Rev Dangerfield, George, 'The Parody of a Hero', Nation CLXXXI
(22 October 1955), 345

Dann, Uriel, 'T.E. Lawrence in Amman, 1921'. Pp. 1-14. Paper read
to the 28th International Congress of Orientalists, Canberra, Australia,
11 January 1971. /In the Imperial War Museum/

B David, Evan, 'Lawrence in the Desert", Great Moments in Adventure,
New York, 1930. Pp. 273-98

Davies, Peter, Ltd., Colonel Lawrence and Others on 'Her Privates We',
London, 1930. /Pamphlet/

Dayton, John, 'Tracking the Train Lawrence Wrecked', Times /London/,
4 December 1964, pp. 13, 22

DeChair, Capt. Somerset, The Golden Carpet, London, 1944

R.D.L.B. /?R.DeLaBere/, 'Aircraftsman, T.E. Shaw', Journal of the R.A.F.
College, Cranwell, XV (Autumn 1935), 178-83

Delorme, Roger, 'La Véritable histoire de Lawrence d'Arabie', Historama, CCIII (septembre 1968), 80-6. See also 87-99

Devas, Nicolette, Two Flamboyant Fathers, New York, 1967. Pp. 90-2

Devers, C. M., 'With Lawrence of Arabia in the Ranks: Personal Recollections of a Private in the Tank Corps', World Today, L (July 1927), 141-4

R ——, 'With Lawrence in the Tank Corps', World's Work, LIV (August 1927), 384-8

De Weerd, Harvey, 'Lawrence', Great Soldiers of the Two World Wars, New York, 1941. Pp. 134-61

——, 'Was Lawrence a Great Soldier?', Cavalry Journal, XLVI (May-June 1937), 268-75

R ——, 'Was Lawrence a Great Soldier?', Infantry Journal, XLIV (1937), 196-204

Dickinson, Hillman, 'Master Guerrilla of Araby's Desert', Army Magazine, XVII (August 1967), 66-7, 70, 72, 76-7

Dinning, Capt. Hector, 'Working With Lawrence', Nile to Aleppo, New York, 1920. Pp. 224-32

Diolé, Philippe, 'Un colonel Shakespearien', Nouvelles littéraires (25 janvier 1962), p. 8

Disbury, David. T.E. Lawrence of Arabia: A Collector's Checklist. Egham, Surrey, 1972

Dixon, Alec, Tinned Soldier: A Personal Record, 1919-1926, London, 1941. Pp. 294-309

Dixon, David, 'Very Superior', Motor Cycle, 3 October 1963, pp. 403-5

Djemal Pasha, Ahmad, 'The Arab Rebellion', Memories of a Turkish Statesman, New York, 1922. Pp. 195-238

Rev Donoghue, Denis, 'London Letter: Moral West End', Hudson Review, XIV (Spring 1961), 97-9

Dooley, Anne, 'My Link with Lawrence of Arabia in Beyond', Two Worlds, 3855 (April 1965), 112-14

Doran, George, Chronicles of Barabbas, 1884-1934, New York, 1952. Pp. 395-7

Doubleday, Frank, 'The Strange Character, Colonel Lawrence', A Few Indiscreet Recollections, n.p. 1928. Pp. 79-88

Dowse, Y.A., 'Lawrence at Clouds Hill', Chambers' Journal, IX (March 1940), 207-8

DuCann, Charles, The Loves of George Bernard Shaw, New York, 1963. Pp. 173-9, 192-3

Duffy, John, 'T.E. Lawrence', 'Arabia Literaria: Four Visions of the East, 1855-1926'. Pp. 257-344. Dissertation Toronto, 1964

*Dunbar, Janet, 'T.E. Lawrence', Mrs. G.B.S.: A Portrait, New York, 1963. Pp. 231-70

Duncan, J.L., 'T.E. Lawrence: Portrait of an Englishman', Dalhousie Review, XXI (April 1941), 71-6

*Duncan, Theodora, 'The Theodora Duncan Collection of T.E. Lawrence', 1968. (Typewritten in the Huntington Library)

———, 'Lawrence - Thirty Years After', Viewpoints, V (May 1965), 15-16

Dunn, G.W.M., 'T.E.', Now and Then, LI (Summer 1935), 7-9

Durrell, Lawrence, Spirit of Place: Letters and Essays on Travel, ed. Alan Thomas, London, 1969. Pp. 33, 133, 139, 141

Duschnes, Philip, Catalogue Number 32: Lawrence of Arabia, New York, 1938

———, 'T.E. Lawrence and Dollars and Sense', Publisher's Weekly, CXXXIV (19 November 1938), 1817-19

*Duval, Elizabeth, T.E. Lawrence: A Bibliography, New York, 1938

Rev Duvignaud, Jean, 'Le colonel bousillé', NRF, XIII (juillet 1965), 113-21

Rev 'New Legends Out of Old', Economist, 233 (4 October 1969), 55

Rev Editor /? Captain De La Bere/, 'A Great Book', R.A.F. Cadet College Magazine, VII (Spring 1927), 24-30

Edmonds, Charles /pseud. of Charles Carrington/, T.E. Lawrence, London, 1935

E./dwards/, J.G., 'T.E. Lawrence', Jesus College Magazine, IV (June 1935), 342-5

Engel, Claire, 'Le Colonel Lawrence et la culture française', Revue de littérature comparée, XX (janvier 1940), 51-65

R ———, Profile anglais: romanciers de guerre, Neuchâtel, 1946. Pp. 127-45

Engel, Anita, 'The Mysterious S.A.', New Statesman, LII (22 December 1956), 812-13

———, 'The Lawrence-Sarah Myth', The Nili Spies, London, 1959. Pp. 229-38

Epstein, Barbara, 'The Legend of T.E. Lawrence: An Astrological Profile', Prediction, XXIX (April 1963), 10-12, 26

Erskine, Mrs Steuart, King Faisal of Iraq, London, 1933

Rev Etiemble, René, 'L'Année T.E. Lawrence', Etudes anglaises, IX (1956), 122-30

Rev ———, 'Chronique littéraire', Les Temps modernes, XXX (mars 1948), 1708-20

Fabre-Luce, A., 'Le Colonel Lawrence et la France', Les Oeuvres libres, 274 (mai 1950), 129-58

Rev Fadiman, Clifton, 'T.E. Lawrence', New Yorker, XI (28 September 1935), 65-8

Rev ———, 'T.E. Lawrence', New Yorker, XV (11 March 1939), 78

Fairbairn, Geoffrey, Revolutionary Warfare and Communist Strategy, London, 1968. Pp. 46, 143-4, 151-5, 201

Rev Fallois, B. de, 'Lawrence le véridique', Revue de Paris, LXII (mars 1955), 128-33

Falls, Cyril, 'Unleashing the Arabs', Armageddon: 1918, New York, 1964. Pp. 100-10

Farber, Stephen, 'Look What They've Done to "Lawrence of Arabia" Now', New York Times, 2 May 1971, sec. 2, p. 11

Fariñas, Enrique, Lawrence de Arabia, Barcelona, 1963

Fedden, Robin, 'T.E. Lawrence', English Travellers in the Near East, London, 1958. Pp. 34-7

——— and John Thomson, Crusader Castles, London, 1957

Feisal, 'Letters from King Feisal to T.E. Lawrence', 1921. (Typewritten, in the British Museum)

B Fellowes-Gordon, Ian, 'T.E. Lawrence', Heroes of the Twentieth Century, New York, 1966. Pp. 144-5

Fernald, Mary. 'The Literary Relationship Between T.E. Lawrence and Mr. and Mrs. Bernard Shaw.' (M.A. thesis) Orono, Maine, 1962

Findlay, Group Capt. Charles, 'T.E. Lawrence: The Amazing AC-2', Listener, LIX (5 June 1958), 937-8

——, 'T.E. Lawrence: The Amazing AC-2', R.A.F. Flying Review, XIII (1958), 30-2

Rev Finley, John, 'Lawrence's Epic of Arabia', New York Times Book Review, 29 September 1935, pp. 1, 15

——, 'Introduction' to T.E. Lawrence's translation of the Odyssey, New York, 1932

Fishman, Jack, My Darling Clementine: The Story of Lady Churchill, New York, 1963. Pp. 71-4

Rev FitzGibbon, Constantine, 'The Lawrence Legend', Encounter, XV (November 1960), 55-6

Rev Fitzsimons, M.A., 'Agonizing Reappraisal of T.E. Lawrence', Commonweal, LXIII (25 November 1955), 202, 204

Flecker, James Elroy, Some Letters From Abroad, London, 1930

Forbes, Rosita. Gypsy in the Sun. London, 1944. Pp. 23, 57-58, 63

Forestier, Marie, The Fort of San Lorenzo, London, 1960

R Forster, E.M., 'Books Abroad', Living Age, 349 (October 1935), 170-4

——, 'Clouds Hill', Listener, XX (1 September 1938), 426-7

R ——, 'Clouds Hill', Two Cheers For Democracy, New York: Harvest, 1951. Pp. 345-8

——, 'Dr. Woolacott'. The Life to Come, London, 1972. Pp. 83-96

Rev ——, 'The Mint by T.E. Lawrence', Listener, LIII (17 February 1955), 279-80

——, 'The Point of It', The Eternal Moment, London, 1928. Pp. 62-92

——, 'T.E.', Listener, XIV (31 July 1935), 211-12

* R ——, 'T.E. Lawrence' /1935/, Abinger Harvest, New York: Meridian, 1955. Pp. 134-40

Foss, Michael. 'Dangerous Guides: English Writers and the Desert', New Middle East, IX (1969), 38-42

Fox, Ralph, 'Lawrence the Twentieth Century Hero', Left Review, I (1935), 391-6

R ——, 'Lawrence the Twentieth Century Hero', Ralph Fox: Writer in Arms, ed. John Lehmann, London, 1937. Pp. 88-95

Frédérix, Pierre, 'T.E. Lawrence', Revue de Paris, LVI (August 1949), 110-25

Friedman, Isaiah. The Question of Palestine, 1914-1918: British-Jewish-Arab Relations. London, 1973

Frost, David, 'Lawrence of Arabia', That Was the Week That Was, Parlophone record, 1963

G /John Gawsworth/, Annotations on Some Minor Writings of T.E. Lawrence, London, 1935

C.G.G., 'Lawrence of Arabia', The Aeroplane, 22 May 1935, p. 588

Gardner, Brian, Allenby of Arabia, Lawrence's General, Intro. by Lowell Thomas, New York, 1965. Pp. 131-44, 187-92, 200-11

Rev Garnett, David, 'Books in General', New Statesmen,   X (27 July 1935), 127

Rev ——, 'Current Literature', New Statesman and Nation, XIII (29 May 1937), 886

——, The Familiar Faces, London, 1962. Pp. 102-13

——, The White-Garnett Letters, New York, 1968. Pp. 55-6, 242, 303-5, 308

Gaster, Z., 'Lawrence and King Hussein; the 1921 Negotiations', National Review, CXI (October 1938), 512-15

Georges-Gaulis, Berthe, Angora, Constantinople, Londres, Paris, 1922. Pp. 220-2

German-Reed, T., Bibliographical Notes on T.E. Lawrence's 'Seven Pillars of Wisdom' and 'Revolt in the Desert', London, 1928

Ghyka, Matila, 'Hamlet en Arabie', Revue de Paris, LXIII (1936), 48-71

Gill, F.C., 'Through a Manse Window', Methodist Magazine, n.v. (July 1949), 322-6

Rev Gillet, Louis, 'El Aruns, ou Lawrence l'Arabe', Revue des deux mondes, XXXIV (août 1936), 688-700

Rev ——, 'L'enigme du Colonel Lawrence', Revue des deux mondes, LIII (15 septembre 1939), 456-70

Glen, Douglas, In the Steps of Lawrence of Arabia, London, 1939

Glubb, Lt.-Gen. Sir John, 'Thomas Edward Lawrence', Encyclopedia Britannica, London, 1967, XIII, 829-30

——, 'The Revolt', Britain and the Arabs: A Study of Fifty Years, 1908-1958, London, 1959. Pp. 79-89

B Golding, Harry, 'Lawrence of Arabia', The Wonder Book of Daring Deeds, London, n.d. Pp. 27-36

Golding, Louis, In the Steps of Moses the Conqueror, London, 1938. Pp. 145-50, 282-4

B Gorman, James. With Lawrence to Damascus, Oxford, 1940. /Pamphlet/

Graham, Colin, 'The Crash Which Killed Lawrence of Arabia', Dorset, II (Summer 1968), 3-5

Graves, Philip, The Life of Sir Percy Cox, London, 1941. Pp. 200-3, 278-84

Graves, Robert, 'Are Women More Romantic Than Men?', Life, LIX (15 October 1965), 135-8

——, 'Children of Darkness', Poems, New York: Anchor, 1958. P. 47

——, 'The Clipped Stater', Poems, 1914-1926, New York, 1929. Pp. 167-70

Rev, R ——, 'Colonel Lawrence's Odyssey', Steps, London, 1958. Pp. 182-8

Rev, R ——, 'Colonel Lawrence's Odyssey', Five Pens in Hand, New York, 1958. Pp. 137-43

* F ——, Good-bye To All That, London: Penguin, 1961. Pp. 242-7

——, 'Introduction' to E.E. Cummings', The Enormous Room, London, 1928. Pp. 7-8

——, 'Isis Idol: Mr. T.E. Lawrence (Arabia and All Souls)', Isis, 567 (27 October 1920), 5

* ——, Lawrence and the Arabian Adventure, New York, 1928. /English edition called Lawrence and the Arabs/

Rev ——, 'Lawrence Vindicated', New Republic, CXXXII (21 March 1955), 16-20

Rev, R ——, 'Lawrence Vindicated', Faces of Five Decades: Selections from Fifty Years of the New Republic, 1914-1964, ed. Robert Luce, New York, 1964. Pp. 346-53

——, 'New Tales About Lawrence of Arabia', World's Work, LV (February 1928), 389-98

——, 'Lawrence of Arabia as a Buck Private', World's Work, LV (March 1928), 508-16

——, 'The Real Col. Lawrence', World's Work, LV (April 1928), 663-70

——, 'The Making of a Conqueror', World's Work, LV (May 1928), 101-11

R ——, 'A Party in the Desert', Adventures and Encounters, eds. E.W. Parker and A.R. Moon, London, 1936. Pp. 152-6

Rev ——, 'No. 2 Polstead Road', New Statesman, XLVIII (24 July 1954), 105-6

——, 'The Pier-Glass', The Pier-Glass, London, 1921. P. 13

Rev ——, 'A Soldier's Homer', New Republic, CXXXV (24 September 1956), 17-19

——, 'T.E. Lawrence and the Riddle of S.A.', Saturday Review, XLVI (15 June 1963), 16-17

—— and Alan Hodge, The Long Weekend: A Social History of Great Britain. 1919-1939, New York: Norton, 1963. Pp. 70-1, 217-19

Great Britain, Egyptian Expeditionary Force, A Brief Record of the Advance of the Egyptian Expeditionary Force Under General Allenby, Cairo, 1919

Gregory, Isabella, Lady Gregory's Journals, ed. Lennox Robinson, London, 1946. Pp. 212-14

Rev Grendzier, Irene, 'Notes on T.E. Lawrence', Middle East Journal, XIX (Spring 1965), 259-61. See also 556-7

Grenier, Roger, 'La Livrée de la Mort', La Table ronde, XCIII (septembre 1955), 131-4

Grindle, Harry, 'The Seven Pillars of Wisdom', Central Literary Magazine, XXXIV (January 1939), 23-30

Gudme, Peter, 'Lawrence af Arabien: Myten, Manden og Strategen' /Myth, Man and Strategist7, Tilskueren /Audience7, II (1938), 372-88

Gullet, Henry, The Australian Imperial Force in Sinai and Palestine, 1914-1918, Sydney, 1923

B Hagedorn, Hermann, 'Lawrence of Arabia', The Book of Courage, Chicago, 1930. Pp. 358-76

Haiber, William, 'To Gain the Rear', Military Review, XLIII (November 1963), 40-9

R, F Halifax, Edward Wood, Lord, 'Lawrence of Arabia', Speeches on Foreign Policy of 1934-1939, London, 1940. Pp. 27-32

F ———, T.E. Lawrence: Address Delivered at St. Paul's Cathedral, 29 June 1936, London, 1936

Hall, Melvin, Journey to the End of an Era: An Autobiography, London, 1948. Pp. 317, 319-21

Hardwick, Michael and Mollie, 'Clouds Hill', Writers' Houses, London, 1968. Pp. 52-6

Rev Hartley, L.P., 'A Failed Masterpiece: The Mint', Listener, LIII (14 April 1955), 658-9

Hassall, Christopher, Edward Marsh: Patron of the Arts, London, 1959. Pp. 530, 539, 544-5

Henderson, Capt. T., 'The Hejaz Expedition, 1916-1917' (1919), 39 pp. /Typescript and photos in the Imperial War Museum7

Henighan, T.J., 'T.E. Lawrence's Seven Pillars of Wisdom: Vision as Pattern', Dalhousie Review, LI (1971), 49-59

Herbert, Aubrey, Mons, Anzac and Kut, London, 1919. Pp. 220, 222, 226, 230, 237

Hergenhan, L.T., 'Some Unpublished Letters from T.E. Lawrence to Frederic Manning', Southerly, XXIII (1963), 242-52

Hill, Margot, 'T.E. Lawrence: Some Trivial Memories', Virginia Quarterly Review, XXI (October 1945), 587-96

Rev H /ogarth7, D.G., 'Review of The Wilderness of Zin', Geographical Journal, XLVI (1915), 55-6

Rev Hogarth, D.G., 'Lawrence of Arabia: Story of His Book', Times /London7, 13 December 1926, pp. 15-16

——, The Life of Charles M. Doughty, London, 1928

——, 'Mecca's Revolt Against the Turks', Century Magazine, LXXVIII (July 1920), 401-11

——, 'T.E. Lawrence', in Twenty Four Portraits by William Rothenstein, First series, London, 1920. No pp

——, 'Thomas Edward Lawrence', Encyclopedia Britannica, 14th ed. London, 1926, XIII, 798-9

Hollings, Frank, ed., Books From the Library of T.E. Lawrence, Catalogue no. 242, London, 1951

Hopkinson, Arthur, Pastor's Progress, London, 1941. Pp. 16-19

Hopkirk, Peter, '£10,000 for Service Papers of Lawrence', Times /London7, 28 September 1971

——, 'Were the Arabs Double-Crossed by Lawrence?', Times /London7, 29 July 1969, p. 6. See also 'Letters' in Times, 31 July and 4 August 1969, pp. 9, 9

——, Fuller, Roy and Parry, Stephen, 'Puzzle of Poems Lawrence Loved', Times /London7, 18 and 19 February 1971, pp. 3 and 15

/Housman, Laurence7, 'Poem', Sur, CLV (julio-octobre 1947), 358-61

*Houston, Guyla Bond, 'Thomas Edward Lawrence: A Checklist of Lawrenciana, 1915-1965'. Typescript, 1967

Howard, Harry, The King-Crane Commission, Beirut, 1963. Pp. 3, 10, 35-6, 43, 71, 92, 266

Howard, Michael, Jonathan Cape, Publisher, London, 1971

Howarth, David, 'Lawrence and the Sherif of Mecca', The Desert King: A Life of Ibn Saud, New York, 1964. Pp. 106-18

Howe, Irving, 'T.E. Lawrence: The Anti-Heroic Hero', Stanford Today, I (Summer 1962), n.p.

* ——, 'T.E. Lawrence: The Problem of Heroism', Hudson Review, XV (1962), 333-64

R ——, 'T.E. Lawrence: The Problem of Heroism', A World More Attractive, New York, 1963. Pp. 1-39

R ——, 'T.E. Lawrence: The Problem of Heroism', Decline of The New, New York, 1970. Pp. 294-326

Rev Hughes, Richard, 'The Lawrence Letters', New Statesman and Nation, XVI (10 December 1938), 1007-8

Rev ——, 'Numen Inest', Spectator, CLV (2 August 1935), 193

Hull, Keith, 'T.E. Lawrence's Perilous Parodies', Texas Quarterly, XV (1972), 56-61

Huxley, Aldous, Letters, ed. Grover Smith, New York, 1969. Pp. 547-8, 558-9, 583n-84

Rev Ireland, Philip, 'Anthony Nutting, Lawrence of Arabia: The Man and the Motive and Robert Payne, Lawrence of Arabia, A Triumph', Middle East Journal, XVIII (Winter 1964), 111-13

Isham, Ralph, 'More Lawrence, Less Legend', Town and Country (November 1935), 43-4

Isherwood, Christopher, The Condor and the Cows, New York, 1949. Pp. 198-99

Rev ——, 'T.E. Lawrence By His Friends', Exhumations, London, 1966. Pp. 22-4

Jackson, Stanley, The Sassoons, New York, 1968. Pp. 178, 186, 223-5, 241-2

Jalabert, Louis, 'Un aventurier et une adventure de grand style: le colonel Lawrence et la révolte arabe', Etudes, VIII (1928), 433-58

Jarché, James, People I Have Shot, London, 1934. Pp. 226-8

Jarvis, Claude, Arab Command: The Biography of Lieutenant-Colonel F.W. Peake Pasha, London, 1942. Pp. 26-54, 78-86

——, 'Lawrence and the Arab Revolt', Three Deserts, London, 1938. Pp. 295-303

Jeffries, J.M.N., Front Everywhere, London, 1935. Pp. 23-7, 239

'Jehanne', Seven Poems Dedicated to T.E. Lawrence, n.p. 1964

——, Ten Poems More Dedicated to T.E. Lawrence, n.p. 1968

John, Augustus, 'Some Letters from Lawrence', Chiaroscuro: Fragments of an Autobiography, New York, 1952. Pp. 244-7

Johns, W.E., 'How Lawrence Joined the R.A.F.', Sunday Times /London/, 8 April 1951, p. 5

Johnson, A.F., 'Aircraftman Shaw', Royal Air Force Review, III (June 1948), 7-8

Jones, Basil, 'Shaw, Formerly Lawrence of Arabia', Popular Flying, IV (August 1935), 259-61, 286

Jones, Thomas, A Diary With Letters, London, 1954. Pp. 143, 149, 173-4, 519-20

'Lawrence of Arabia', Journal of the Society of Film and Television Arts, X (Winter 1962-3), 1-24

Joyce, Colonel P.C., 'Two BBC Broadcasts on Lawrence', 30 August 1939 and 14 July 1941, 6 pp. /Typescript in the Imperial War Museum/

Jullian, Philippe, Flight Into Egypt: A Fantasy, New York, 1970

Kadmi-Cohen, 'Deux grands coloniaux anglais, Lawrence et Philby', Mercure de France, CCXXIX (1 August 1931), 576-94

Kashani, Jamal, 'S.A. - The Spy in T.E.'s Life', Iran Tribune, 14 March 1969, p. 47

Kearsey, Lt.-Col. A., A Summary of the Strategy and Tactics of the Egypt and Palestine Campaign, 1917-1918, Aldershot, 193-. Pp. 9, 93

Kedourie, Elie, 'The Capture of Damascus, 1 October 1918', Middle Eastern Studies, I (October 1964), 66-83

R ——, 'The Capture of Damascus, 1 October 1918', The Chatham House Version, London, 1970. Pp. 33-51. See also 13-32, 236-82

——, 'Colonel Lawrence', Cambridge Journal, VII (June 1954), 515-30

R ——, 'Colonel Lawrence', England and the Middle East: The Destruction of the Ottoman Empire, 1914-1921 London, 1956. Pp. 88-106

B Kennet, John, Prince Dynamite, London, 1952

Kennet, Lady, Self Portrait of an Artist , London, 1949. Pp. 125, 188-190, 246-247, 268, 295-296, 302-303, 359

F Kennington, Eric, 'Lawrence: An Unofficial Portrait', Atlantic Monthly, CLIX (April 1937), 406-15

Kent, Howard, Single Bed for Three: A Lawrence of Arabia Notebook, London, 1963

Kenyon, Sir Frederick, 'The Wilderness of Zin: A Preface', Now and Then, LIII (Spring 1936), 29-30

Kern, Edward, 'The Desert Revolt Urged on by a Legendary Englishman', Life, LXIII (20 October 1967), 54-8

B Kiernan, Reginald, Lawrence of Arabia, London, 1935

Kimche, Jon, Seven Fallen Pillars: The Middle East. 1915-1950, London, 1953

King, R.F., 'Another Lawrence: Aircraftman Shaw and Air-Cushion Aircraft', Air-Cushion Vehicles, VII (February 1966), 19-23

Kinross, Lord /J.P.D. Balfour7, 'Aircraftman Shaw', Royal Air Force College Journal, II (March 1944), 82-3

Kirby, H.T., 'Lawrence of Arabia - Brass Rubber', Apollo, XXVIII (July 1938), 18-19

Kirkbride, Sir Alec, An Awakening: The Arab Campaign, 1917-18, Tavistock, Devon, 1971

——, 'T.E. Lawrence: A Memory of the Hedjaz, 1918', Manchester Guardian, 20 August 1956, pp. 4, 6

——, 'T.E. Lawrence', A Crackle of Thorns: Experiences in the Near East, London, 1956. Pp. 5-11

Rev Kirstein, Lincoln, 'Letters of T.E. Lawrence', Nation, CXLIX (8 July 1939), 47-8

Kittridge, Helen, 'The Wayfarer': A Dramatization of Seven Chapters of the Odyssey, According to the Translation of T.E. Shaw, Los Angeles, 1935

Klieman, Aaron, Foundations of British Policy in the Arab World: The Cairo Conference of 1921, Baltimore, 1970. Pp. 107-9, 221-7

*Knight, G. Wilson, 'T.E. Lawrence', Neglected Powers, New York, 1971. Pp. 53-7, 309-51

Knightley, Phillip and Simpson, Colin, 'Lawrence: The End of a Legend', Sunday Times /London7, 31 August, 7 and 14 September 1969, pp. 21-2, 45-6, 49-50

——, 'The Secret Life of Lawrence of Arabia', Sunday Times /London/, 9, 16, 23, 30 June 1968, pp. 49-50, 49-50, 45-46, 45-6

* ——, The Secret Lives of Lawrence of Arabia, New York, 1970

——, 'Aldington's Enquiry Concerning T.E. Lawrence', Texas Quarterly, XVI (1973), 98-105

Knowles, John, 'All-Out in the Desert', Horizon, IV (July 1962), 108-11

Kolisko, Eugen, 'Reincarnation: Lawrence of Arabia', Modern Mystic, II (August 1938), 298-301

B Komroff, Manuel, 'Prince Dynamite', True Adventures of Spies, Boston, 1954. Pp. 109-27

Kressenstein, Col. Baron Friedrich Kress von, 'The Campaign in Palestine - from the Enemy's Side', Journal of the Royal United Service Institution, LXVII (August 1922), 503-13

Kutay, Cemal, Lavrens 'E Karşi Kuşcubaşi /Kuşcubaşi Against Lawrence/, Istanbul, 1965

J.D.L., 'T.E. Lawrence - Another Point of View', Spectator, CXCV (9 July 1955), 42

Laar, Klemens, Kampf in der Wüste, Berlin, 1938

Rev LaBadie, Donald, 'The Reel Lawrence', Show, III (March 1963), 31

LaCour, Paul, 'En uhaandterlig Krystal' /An Unmanageable Crystal/, Tilkueren /Audience/, I (1937), 102-11

Lacouture, Jean, 'T.E. Lawrence'. André Malraux: Une Vie dans la siècle. Paris, 1973. Pp. 201-208

Laird, J.T., 'T.E. Lawrence: The Problem of Interpretation', Australian Quarterly (March 1960), 93-9

Lawrence, New York: Dell Comic Book, 1963

Lawrence, A.W., 'The Fiction and the Fact', Observer, 16 December 1962, p. 25

R ——, 'Brother Rejects Film on Lawrence', New York Times International Edition, 12 January 1963, p. 5

——, 'Introduction to The Mint', Sunday Times /London/, 23 January 1955, p. 6

———, 'T.E. Lawrence: A Brother Gives His Testimony', Times /London7, 22 November 1969, p. 7

* ———, ed. Letters to T.E. Lawrence, London, 1962

* ———, ed., T.E. Lawrence By His Friends, London, 1937

Lawrence, T.E. /pseud.7, 'Nile Mother and Mistress', American Aphrodite, I (1951), 64-9

Rev Lazare, Christopher, 'Ornament of Honour', Nation, CXLV (25 September 1937), 328-9

Lean, David, 'Out of the Wilderness', Films and Filming, IX (January 1963), 12-15

Rev Leibovici, Marcel, 'T.E. Lawrence: La Matrice', La Nouvelle N.R.F., XXXI (juillet 1955), 144-6

Lengyel, Emil, 'Lawrence of Arabia', World Without End: The Middle East, New York, 1953. Pp. 104-18

Levi Della Vida, G., 'L'Arabia di Lawrence', Cultura, IX (1930), 352-66

Lewington, H.W. with Schulze, Kurt, With Colonel Lawrence in the Arab Revolt, n.p., 1936

Rev Lewis, C. Day, 'T.E. Lawrence', Spectator, CLXI (25 November 1938), 908

*Lewis, Wyndham, 'Lawrence of Arabia', Blasting and Bombardiering: An Autobiography, 1914-1926, London, 1937. Pp. 241-8

———, 'Perspectives on Lawrence', Hudson Review, VIII (Winter 1956), 596-608

Liddell Hart, B.H., 'Allenby of Megiddo: The Evolution of a Leader', Reputations: Ten Years After, Boston, 1928. Pp. 233-60

* ———, Colonel Lawrence, the Man Behind the Legend, New York, 1935 /English edition called T.E. Lawrence: In Arabia and After7

———, 'Lawrence: The Artist in War and Letters', Lawrence of Arabia, London, 1936. N.p.

———, 'Lawrence of Arabia', Times /London7, 20 May 1935, pp. 15-16

R ———, 'Lawrence of Arabia', Saturday Review of Literature, XII (22 June 1935), 3-4, 15

———, 'Lawrence of Arabia', TLS, 3 November 1961, p. 789

———, 'Lawrence of Arabia, the (Almost) Free Man', Men of Turmoil, New York, 1935. Pp. 99-112. /English edition called Great Contemporaries/

———, Memoirs, London, 1965, I, 339-56

* Rev ———, 'T.E. Lawrence, Aldington and the Truth', London Magazine, II (April 1955), 67-75

———, 'Reply by Aldington and Answer by Liddell-Hart', London Magazine, II (August 1955), 66-71

———, Strategy: The Indirect Approach, London, 1967. Pp. 197-200

R ———, 'T.E. Lawrence: Man or Myth?', Atlantic Monthly, CXCVI (November 1955), 70-6

———, 'T.E. Lawrence: Through His Own Eyes and Another's', Southern Review, II (1936), 22-40

Liman Von Sanders, General Otto, Five Years in Turkey, Annapolis, 1927

Lipton, Dean, 'The Lawrence of Arabia Myth', Nexus, I (August 1963), 1-11

'Four Best Selling Personalities', Literary Digest, CXXI (11 January 1936), 28

Rev Lloyd, Lord George, 'Seven Pillars', National Review, CV (September 1935), 342-6

Lloyd-George, David, The Truth About the Peace Treaties, London, 1938. Vol.II, 1021, 1028, 1035, 1038-40. /American edition called Memoirs of the Peace Conference/

B Longman, M.E., 'The Arab Revolt', Fifty Mutinies, Rebellions and Revolutions, London, n.d. Pp. 561-71

* Lönnroth, Erik, Lawrence of Arabia: An Historical Appreciation, London, 1956

———, 'Thomas Edward Lawrence', En annan uppfattning /Another Interpretation/, Stockholm, 1949. Pp. 190-207

Lord, John, Duty, Honor, Empire: The Life and Times of Colonel Richard Meinertzhagen, New York, 1970. Pp. 336-41, 355-7

Rev Lovelock, R.C.O., 'The Mint – and the Metal: T.E. Lawrence's Life in the R.A.F.', Flight, LXVII (18 March 1955), 356

Rev Lucas-Dubreton, J., 'La Vie aventureuse du Colonel Lawrence', Revue des deux mondes, XXVIII (juillet 1935), 168-9

Lührs, Hans, Gegenspieler des Obersten Lawrence, Berlin, 1936

Lunt, Lt-Col. J.D., 'An Unsolicited Tribute', Blackwood's Magazine, 277 (April 1955), 289-96

——, 'Los arabes y Lawrence', Historia Mundial del Siglo 20, XXII (1971), 43-8

'Romantic Riddle', MD, IV (April 1960), 221-7

MacDonald, Philip, The List of Adrian Messenger, New York, 1959

R. Mack, John, 'The Inner Conflict of T.E. Lawrence', Times /London/, 8 February 1969, p. 17

* ——, 'T.E. Lawrence: A Study in Heroism and Conflict', American Journal of Psychiatry, CXXV (February 1969), 1083-92. 'Correspondence' (May 1969), 1604-9

MacLean, Alistair, Lawrence of Arabia, New York, 1962

MacLean, Hugh, 'T.E. Lawrence: Hero', Queen's Quarterly, LX (1953), 367-83

MacLean, James, 'Lawrence of Arabia', London Scottish Regimental Gazette, LXIV (December 1959), 218-21

MacLean, Norman, 'They Won the War', His Terrible Swift Sword, London, 1942. Pp. 73-7

MacLeish, Archibald, 'Speech to the Detractors' /1936/, Collected Poems, 1917-1952, Boston, 1952. Pp. 103-4. See also p. 327

MacMunn, Lt.-General Sir George, 'The Truth About T.E. Lawrence', World Today, L (1927), 559-64

—— and Falls, Captain Cyril, 'The Arab Campaign', Military Operations, Egypt and Palestine, London, 1928-30. I. 205-41 II, 395-410, 563-7, 582-94

C.K.S. /Lt-General Sir George MacMunn/, 'The Uncrowned King of Arabia', Sphere, CII (8 August 1925), 185

Macphail, Andrew, 'Colonel Lawrence', Three Persons, London, 1929.
   Pp. 195-235

MacVeagh, Charles, 'A Figure in the Tapestry of Dreams: A Study of T.E.
   Lawrence', Harvard Honors thesis, 1953

Malraux, André, Antimemoirs, New York, 1968. Pp. 4, 8, 54, 64-5,
   74, 258

——, 'Lawrence'. Panorama de la nouvelle littérature française. ed.
   Gaeton Picon. Paris, 1949. Pp. 298-304

——, 'The Demon of the Absolute: A Study of T.E. Lawrence', World
   Review, II (August, October 1949), 9-12, 33-7

* R ——, 'Lawrence and the Demon of the Absolute', Hudson Review,
   VIII (1956), 519-32

* ——, The Walnut Trees of Altenburg, London, 1952

Rev Marion, Denis, 'Un Illustre inconnu: T.E. Lawrence', Critique,
   CIV (1956), 52-61

Marlowe, John. Late Victorian: The Life of Sir Arnold Wilson. London,
   1967

Marsh, Sir Edward, A Number of People: A Book of Reminiscences,
   London, 1939. Pp. 234-9, 344-5

——, 'A Number of People', Harper's, CLXXIX (July 1939), 173-4

Martenson, Börje, Lawrence av Arabien, ?Helsingfors, ?1944

Matte, Marcel, 'Un témoin dépose: La vérité sur Lawrence d'Arabie',
   Nouvelles littéraires, 14 mars 1963, pp. 1, 10

Maugham, Robin, Nomad, New York, 1948. Pp. 49-53, 83, 133, 200

Mayer, Emile, 'Du Colonel Lawrence à la guerre italo-éthiopienne',
   Grande revue, XL (1936), 188-98

McCance, William, 'Lawrence: R.I.P.', Picture Post, VI (6 January
   1940), 12-14

McKenny, Harold, 'T.E. Lawrence and the Arabian Revolt, 1914-1918',
   B.A. thesis Illinois, 1953

Mee, Arthur, Dorset: Thomas Hardy's Country, London, 1945. Pp. 165-8

* Meinertzhagen, Colonel Richard, <u>Army Diary, 1899-1926</u>, London, 1960. Pp. 212-27, 283-7

* ——, <u>Middle East Diary, 1917-1956</u>, London, 1959. Pp. 27-43, 95-9, 117-18

Meulenijzer, Victor, <u>Le Colonel Lawrence, agent de l'Intelligence Service</u>, Paris, 1938

* Meyers, Jeffrey, 'T.E. Lawrence', <u>Bulletin of Bibliography</u>, XXIX (January-March 1972), 25-36

* ——, 'E.M. Forster and T.E. Lawrence: A Friendship'. <u>South Atlantic Quarterly</u>, LXIX (Spring 1970), 205-16

* ——, 'Nietzsche and T.E. Lawrence', <u>Midway</u>, XI (Summer 1970), 77-85

* ——, 'The Revisions of <u>Seven Pillars of Wisdom</u>', <u>PMLA</u> LXXXVIII (October 1973), 1066-82

* ——, 'The Secret Lives of Lawrence of Arabia', <u>Commonweal</u>, XCIII (23 October 1970), 100-4

Rev ——, '<u>The Secret Lives of Lawrence of Arabia</u>', <u>Boston Globe</u>, 7 May 1970, p. 39

——, 'T.E. Lawrence', <u>The Idealist in Politics</u>. New York: 1975

* ——, 'The Wounded Spirit: A Study of "Seven Pillars of Wisdom" ', London: Martin, Brian & O'Keeffe, 1973

Meynell, Viola, ed. <u>The Best of Friends: Further Letters to Sir Sydney Cockerell</u>, London, 1956

——, 'T.E. Lawrence', <u>Friends of a Lifetime: Letters to Sir Sydney Carlyle Cockerell</u>, London, 1940. Pp. 357-73

Millar, Ronald, <u>Kut: The Death of an Army</u>, Boston, 1970. Pp. 252-3, 270-5

Miller, Alice, 'Guest on the Staircase at Raynham', <u>I Have Loved England</u>, New York, 1941. N.p.

* Mills, Gordon, 'T.E. Lawrence as a Writer', <u>Texas Quarterly</u>, V (1962), 35-45

Milne, James, 'T.E. Lawrence in Buchan: A Little Known Episode', <u>Buchan Club: Transactions</u>, XVII (1954), 15-21

Miquel, André, 'Quand un Arabe juge Lawrence', Critique, XIX (November 1963), 946-57

Monroe, Elizabeth, Britain's Moment in the Middle East, 1914-1956, London, 1963

——, Philby of Arabia. London, 1973

——, 'The Round Table and the Middle Eastern Peace Settlement, 1917-1922', Round Table, LX (November 1970), 479-90

Moore, Harry, 'Richard Aldington in His Last Years', Texas Quarterly, VI (Autumn 1963), 63, 66-8

R ——, Richard Aldington: An Intimate Portrait, eds., Alister Kershaw and F.J. Temple, Carbondale, Illinois, 1966. Pp. 86-8, 93-4

Mossuz, Janine, André Malraux et le Gaullisme . Paris, 1970. Pp. 275-283

Mountfort, Guy, 'In the Footsteps of T.E. Lawrence', Portrait of a Desert: The Story of an Expedition to Jordan, Boston, 1965. Pp. 123-34

* Mousa, Suleiman, T.E. Lawrence: An Arab View, London, 1966

Mousa, Suleiman, 'The Role of the Syrians and the Iraqis in the Arab Revolt', Middle East Forum, XLIII (1967), 5-17

Mrazerk, Col. James, 'The Philosophy of the Guerrilla Fighter', Army Quarterly and Defence Journal, XCVI (April 1968), 64-74

Rev Muggeridge, Malcolm, 'Poor Lawrence', New Statesman, LXII (27 October 1961), 604-6

B Mundy, Talbot, Jimgrim and Allah's Peace, New York, 1936

Munsey, Jack, 'The "Selves" of T.E. Lawrence as Revealed in Seven Pillars of Wisdom', M.A. thesis, Cornell, 1963

Nadeau, N., 'T.E. Lawrence: valet de chambre de l'idéal', Mercure de France, CCCVI (May 1949), 124-8

Nakano, Yoshio, Arabia no Rorensu /Lawrence of Arabia7, Tokyo, 1940

F Namier, Lewis, 'Lawrence as a Friend', Living Age, CCCXLVIII (July 1935), 421-6

——, 'T.E. Lawrence', In the Margin of History, London, 1939. Pp. 273-304

National Trust, Clouds Hill, London, 1970

Nedden, Otto, T.E. Lawrence (Lawrence von Arabien); die Legende seines Lebens für die Bühne gestaltet, Barmen-Wuppertal, 1958

Nelson, Nina, Shepheard's Hotel, New York, 1961. Pp. 86-7, 89-90

Nevakivi, Jukka, Britain, France and the Arab Middle East, 1914-1920, London, 1969

Nevins, Edward and Wright, Theon, World Without Time, New York, 1969

Newcombe, Col. S.F., 'T.E. Lawrence: Personal Reminiscences', Palestine Exploration Fund. Quarterly Statement, LXVII (July, October 1935), 110-13, 162-4

'The Sound and the Silence of T.E. Lawrence', News Front, XIV (Midsummer, September 1970), 46-7, 16-17

Nickerson, Hoffman, 'Lawrence and Future Generalship', American Review, VI (December 1935), 129-54

Nitschke, August, 'Politik im Dienst der Abstraktion: Thomas Edward Lawrence', Der Feind, Stuttgart, 1964. Pp. 163-93

Nogales, Gen. Rafael de, 'Emir Feizal's Liberating Army', Memoirs of a Soldier of Fortune, New York, 1932. Pp. 347-55

Norton, Capt. John, 'I Flew Lawrence in War-Crazed Arabia', Liberty, XI (20, 27 January, 3, 10 February 1934), 5-10, 22-7, 47-51, 42-7

* Notopoulos, James, 'The Tragic and the Epic in T.E. Lawrence', Yale Review, LIV (Spring 1965), 331-45

Nouri Al-Said, 'Revolt in the Desert: Introduction to the Arabic Version', Near East and India, XXXI (28 April 1927), 496-7

Nutting, Anthony, Lawrence of Arabia, New York, 1961

Ocampo, Victoria, 338171 T.E. Lawrence of Arabia, Intro. by A.W. Lawrence, New York, 1963

——, 'El Aurens en el desierto de la Pantalla', Sur, 284 (septiembre-octubre 1963), 22-36

——, 'Propositos de Lawrence de Arabia', Sur, 282 (mayo-junio 1963), 1-2

* O'Donnell, Thomas, 'The Dichotomy of Self in T.E. Lawrence's Seven Pillars of Wisdom', Dissertation Illinois, 1970

Oxford High School for Boys, Proceedings at the Unveiling of the Memorial of Lawrence of Arabia, 3 October 1936, Oxford, 1937

Papen, Franz von, Memoirs, London, 1952. Pp. 68-83

Patch, Blanche, 'Lawrence of Arabia', Thirty Years With G.B.S., London, 1951. Pp. 76-87

Patton, Major Oliver, 'Colonel T.E. Lawrence of Arabia', Military Review, XXXIV (October 1954), 18-21

Pavey, R.A., 'The Arab Revolt', Marine Corps Gazette, XL (July 1956), 48-52

Payne, Robert, Lawrence of Arabia, New York, 1962

———, A Portrait of André Malraux, Englewood Cliffs, N.J., 1970. Pp. 296-300

Pearl, Jack, 'Lawrence of Arabia', Impact, XIII (February 1964), 60-74

Penzer, Norman, An Annotated Bibliography of Sir Richard Burton, London, 1923. Pp. 7, 9

Petit, D. Pastor, 'La vida y el mito de T.E. Lawrence', Destino, 6 marzo 1965, pp. 28-31

Philby, H.A.R., 'Lawrence of Arabia', Review of Reviews, LXXXVI (June 1935), 15-17

Philby, Harry St John, Arabian Days: An Autobiography, London, 1948

Rev ———, 'Col. Lawrence's Book', Observer, 13 March 1927, p. 9

* ———, 'T.E. Lawrence and His Critics', Forty Years in the Wilderness, London, 1957. Pp. 82-109

Preston, Lt.-Col. R.M., The Desert Mounted Corps, Boston, 1923. Pp. 130, 195, 255, 257, 278

Pridham, Llewellyn, 'Lawrence of Arabia: A Man of Mystery', Dorset Year Book (1952-3), pp. 113-17

Prince, A.E., 'Lawrence of Arabia', Queen's Quarterly, XLII (August 1935), 366-77

Pritchett, V.S., 'A Portrait of T.E. Lawrence', <u>Books in General</u>, London, 1953. Pp. 37-42

Rev ——, 'Ross at the Depot', <u>The Living Novel</u>, New York: Vintage, 1967. Pp. 288-93

Procopio, Frank, 'The Gentle Assassins', <u>Infantry Magazine</u>, LVI (September-October 1966), 51-5

Rattigan, Col. Clive, 'Lawrence the Soldier', <u>Saturday Review</u>, CLVII (31 March 1934), 350

* Rattigan, Terence, <u>Ross</u>, London, 1960

—— and Grunwald, Anatole, 'Lawrence of Arabia' /screenplay, not filmed7, 1960

Read, Herbert, <u>English Prose Style</u>, Boston: Beacon, 1952. Pp. 195, 205-6

* Rev ——. 'Lawrence of Arabia' and '<u>The Seven Pillars of Wisdom</u>', <u>A Coat of Many Colours</u>, London, 1956. Pp. 19-26

Rev ——, 'Letters to T.E. Lawrence', <u>Listener</u>, LXVIII (16 July 1962), 145

R ——, 'The Seven Pillars of Wisdom', <u>The Bibliophiles' Almanack for 1928</u>, London, 1928. Pp. 35-41

Reiffer, A.H.R., 'Recollections of Life in the Tank Corps 1916-18 and of T.E. Lawrence 1923-25'. (Typewritten, in the Imperial War Museum)

Rensburg, J.F.J. van, 'Lawrence of Arabia', <u>Commando</u>, XIV (1963), 40-3

Rhys, Ernest, 'Colonel T.E. Lawrence', <u>Letters From Limbo</u>, London, 1936. Pp. 145-7

Rice, Howard, Jr., 'Additions to the Doubleday Collection: T.E. Lawrence', <u>Princeton University Library Chronicle</u>, XXIV (Spring 1963), 193-5

Rich, Barbara /pseud. of Robert Graves and Laura Riding7, <u>No Decency Left</u>, London, 1932. Pp. 153-5

* Richards, Vyvyan, <u>Portrait of T.E. Lawrence</u>, London, 1936

R ——, <u>T.E. Lawrence</u>, London, 1939

Riding, Laura, 'The Cult of Failure: Rimbaud', <u>Epilogue</u>, I (1935), 65-6

Rivington, Annabella. <u>Poems</u> . London: privately printed, 1973

Roberts, Chalmers, 'Lawrence of Arabia', World Today, XLIX (April 1927), 417, 441-5

B Robinson, Edward, 'Lawrence of Arabia', Achievement: A Book of Modern Enterprise, ed. Jocelyn Oliver, London, 1937. Pp. 243-9

B ——, Lawrence the Rebel, London, 1946

B ——, Lawrence: The Story of His Life, Oxford, 1935

Rodd, Sir James Rennell, Social and Diplomatic Memories. (Third Series) 1902-1919. London, 1925. Pp. 383-384

Rodman, Selden, Lawrence, the Last Crusade: A Dramatic Narrative Poem, New York, 1937

Rogers, Bruce, Paragraphs on Printing, New York, 1943. Pp. 148-60

——, Pi: Letters, Papers, Addresses, New York, 1953. Pp. 51-2, 68-9, 73-4

Rolls, Sam C., Steel Chariots in the Desert, London, 1937. Pp. 151-286

Roodes, B.H., T.E. Lawrence: Il Re Senza Corona, Milano, 1935

Roosevelt, Kermit, War in the Garden of Eden, London, 1920. Pp. 201-4

Roseler, David /pseud. of E.V. Timms7, Lawrence, Prince of Mecca, Sydney, 1927

Rev Rosenberg, Harold, 'The Hero of Arabia', Poetry, L (August 1937), 285-9

* Rota, Bertram, 'Lawrence of Arabia and Seven Pillars of Wisdom', Texas Quarterly, V (1962), 46-53

Rothenstein, John, Summer's Lease: Autobiography, 1901-1938, London, 1965. Pp. 64-72

Rothenstein, William, Since Fifty: Men and Memories, 1922-1938, London, 1939. Pp. 8-12, 69-72, 83-4, 104-6, 263-6

Rougemont, Denis de, 'Prototype T.E.L.', Dramatic Personages, New York, 1964. Pp. 135-51

'T.E. Lawrence and the Streets in the Tropics', Royal Institute of British Architects Journal, XLIII (7 December 1935), 116

Sacher, Howard, 'The Declining World of T.E. Lawrence', New Republic, CXXX (10 May 1954), 18-19

——, The Emergence of the Middle East, 1914-1924, New York, 1969

St Paul's Cathedral, Form of Service Used at the Unveiling of the Memorial to Thomas Edward Lawrence, London, 1936

Rev Salanova, Cécile, 'Lawrence d'Arabie: Du mythe à la realité', Plexus, XXXV (mai 1970), 24-36

Sanders, Frederick, 'Lawrence of Arabia', 1938. (Typewritten, in the British Museum)

Sassoon, Siegfried, Siegfried's Journey, 1916-1920, New York, 1946. Pp. 128-31

Savage, Raymond, Allenby of Armageddon, Indianapolis, 1926

Scannell, Vernon, 'Any Complaints?', The Oxford Book of Twentieth Century English Verse. ed. Philip Larkin, Oxford, 1973. Pp. 545-546

Schroers, Rolf, T.E. Lawrence: Schicksal und Gestalt: Biographische Studie, Bremen, 1949

Scott, Kathleen /Lady Kennet/, Homage: A Book of Sculptures, London, 1930. Plate XXV & 3 pp.

Scott-James, R.A., The Day Before Yesterday, London, 1947. Pp. 35-6

——, Fifty Years of English Literature, London, 1951. Pp. 190-2

Sejersted, Georg, Lawrence og Hans Arabere, Oslo, 1936

Serez, ÖmerNaci, T.E. Lawrence ve Arap Isyani /T.E. Lawrence and the Arab Revolution/, Istanbul, 1965

Shahani, Major, 'Lawrence of Arabia', United States of India Journal (July-September 1966)

Shahbender, Abdul, 'Lawrence in the Balance', Al-Muqtataf /Cairo/, (March-July 1931)

Rev Shanks, Edward, 'The Greatest Adventure', Saturday Review, CXLIII (12 March 1927), 396

Rev Shaw, G.B., 'The Latest from Colonel Lawrence', Spectator, CXXXVIII (12 March 1927), 429

* R ——, 'The Man Lawrence', World's Work, LIII (April 1927), 636-8

R ——, 'Revolt in the Desert and Its Author', Now and Then, XXXIII (Spring 1927), 20-2

R ——, 'Revolt in the Desert and Its Author', Then and Now, London, 1935, Pp. 127-31

——, Saint Joan, London, 1923

——, Too True To Be Good, London, 1934

Rev Sheean, Vincent, 'T.E. Lawrence: A Revelation and a Miracle', New York Herald Tribune Book Review, 29 September 1935, pp. 1-2

Sherwood, Jane, Post-Mortem Journal: Communications from T.E. Lawrence, London, 1964

Sherwood, John, No Golden Journey: A Biography of James Elroy Flecker. London, 1973. Pp. xiii, 34, 146-148, 151-152

Shiftah, Nasr Allah, Sih mard-i 'ajib /Three Strange Men7, Teheran, 1947

Sholl, Anna, 'Lawrence of Arabia', Catholic World, CXLI (August 1935), 532

Shotwell, James, At the Paris Peace Conference, New York, 1937. Pp. 131-2, 197

Shumway, Harry, War in the Desert, Glasgow, 1938. /American edition called Lawrence, the Arabian Knight7

Siegel, Larry, 'Flawrence of Arabia', Mad Magazine, LXXXVI (April 1964), 43-8

Simon, John, 'Rattigan Talks', Theater Arts, XLVI (April 1962), 23-4, 72

Rev ——, 'Theater Chronicle', Hudson Review, XV (Spring 1962), 117

B Slade, Gurney /pseud. of Stephen Bartlett7, In Lawrence's Bodyguard, New York, 1930

B ——, Lawrence in the Blue, New York, 1936

B ——, Led by Lawrence, New York, 1934

Small, Alex, 'Colonel Lawrence and the Afghan Revolt', China Weekly Review, XLVII (23 February 1929), 527

Smith, A.W., 'Lawrence and Clive', Atlantic Monthly, CLVII(April 1936), 447-56

Smith, Clare Sydney, The Golden Reign: The Story of My Friendship With T.E. Lawrence, London, 1940

Smith, Janet, John Buchan, London, 1965. Pp. 207n, 224, 236, 241-4, 262-3, 280, 326-7, 379

Smyth, Ethel, 'Letters from T.E. Shaw to M.B.', Maurice Baring, London, 1938. Pp. 337-9

Sotheby & Co., 'An Important Collection of Books and Letters, by or Relating to T.E. Lawrence', Modern First Editions, London, 10 December 1968. Pp. 102-13. See also 11-12 March 1968

Spens, Willy de, Les Gazelles royales d'Arabie, Paris, 1964

* Sperber, Manes, 'False Situations: T.E. Lawrence and His Two Legends', The Achilles Heel, London, 1959. Pp. 175-204

Stallybrass, Oliver, 'Introduction' to E.M. Forster's The Life to Come, London, 1972. Pp. vii-xxi

Steffens, Lincoln, "'Americans are Impossible': An Interview with Lawrence of Arabia", Outlook, CLIX (14 October 1931), 203-5, 222-4

* Stéphane, Roger ⟨pseud. of Roger Worms⟩, Portrait de l'aventurier: T.E. Lawrence, Malraux et von Salomon, Introduction by Jean-Paul Sartre, Paris, 1950

——, T.E. Lawrence, Paris, 1960

Stewart, Philip, 'Another Lawrence Myth', Middle East Forum, XXXIX (June 1963), 17-18

* Stirling, Lt.-Col. Walter, Safety Last: An Autobiography, London, 1953

——, 'Tales of Lawrence of Arabia', Cornhill Magazine, LXXIV (April 1933), 494-510

Storrs, Ronald, 'Das Retrospective Gepack: Maurice Baring and T.E. Lawrence', English, VIII (Autumn 1950), 112-16

——, 'Introduction' to Eric Kennington's Drawing the R.A.F.: A Book of Portraits, New York, 1942. Pp. 11-32

* ——, 'Lawrence', Orientations, London, 1937. Pp. 517-32 ⟨American edition called The Memoirs of Sir Ronald Storrs⟩

R ——, 'Lawrence of Arabia', Lawrence of Arabia. Zionism and Palestine, Harmondsworth, 1940

——, 'Lawrence: Himself', Lawrence of Arabia, London, 1936. N.p.

Rev ——, 'Lawrence of Arabia', Listener, LIII (3 February 1955), 187-9

——, 'The Spell of Arabia: Charles Doughty and T.E. Lawrence', Listener, XXXVIII (25 December 1947), 1093-4

——, 'T.E. Lawrence', Sixteen Portraits of People Whose Homes Have Been Preserved By the National Trust, ed. Leonard Strong, London, 1951. Pp. 110-22

F, R ——, 'T.E. Lawrence - The Man', London Calling, XXXV (22 June 1940), 1-2

——, 'Thomas Edward Lawrence', Dictionary of National Biography, 1931-1940, London, 1949. Pp. 528-31

Suffert, Georges, 'Lawrence, homme fasciste ou athée parfait', Les Mal pensants, IX (1951), 272-85

Sugarman, Sidney, 'The Truth about T.E. Lawrence and the Arab Revolt', Jewish Observer and Middle East Review (12 September 1969), Pp. 17-20

Sulzberger, C.L., 'Foreign Affairs: Giap of Arabia', New York Times, 22 March 1968, p. 46

Sur, CCXXXV (julio-agosto 1955), 1-72. /Special issue on Lawrence7

Sutherland, L.W. and Ellison, Norman, 'Our Lawrence', Aces and Kings, Sydney, 1935. Pp. 71-113

Swaffer, Hannen, 'Debunking Lawrence of Arabia', Literary Digest, CXV (22 April 1933), 15

* Sykes, Christopher, 'Introduction' to Richard Aldington's Lawrence of Arabia, London, 1969. Pp. 2-10

Rev ——, 'Mystery Motorist', Spectator, CCIX (20 July 1962), 89

——, Nancy: The Life of Lady Astor, London, 1972. Pp. 308-11, 315, 349, 353, 360-1, 513-14, 520

——, Orde Wingate: A Biography, New York, 1959

Symons, Julian, 'T.E. Lawrence', Sunday Times Magazine /London7, 29 January 1967, p. 23

Tabachnick, Stephen. 'Two 'Arabian' Romantics: Charles Doughty and T.E. Lawrence', English Literature in Transition, XVI (1973), 11-25

Taylor, Alan and Lydia, 'A Reminiscence of Lawrence: The Story of Fareedah Akle', Viewpoints, IV (November 1964), 22-4

Taylor, Theodore, People Who Make Movies, New York, 1967. Pp. 11, 16, 29-30, 88-9

Templewood, Viscount /Samuel Hoare/, Empire of the Air, London, 1957. Pp. 255-8

Testimonios-Sur, Septima Serie, 1962-7. Buenos Aires, 1967. Pp. 63-118

Thomas, John, The True Book About Lawrence, London, 1953

B Thomas, Lowell, Boy's Life of Colonel Lawrence, London, 1927

——, 'I Remember Lawrence of Arabia', TV Guide, XXI (27 January 1973), 19-21

Rev ——, 'Lawrence of Arabia: A Biographical Enquiry by Richard Aldington', Middle East Journal, IX (Spring 1955), 197-8

——, 'Lawrence of Arabia: Who He Was and What He Did', World's Work, LIII-LIV (February, April, June 1927), 362-8, 639-42, 184-96

——, 'The Real Lawrence of Arabia', Reader's Digest, June 1964, pp. 252-65, 271-4

——, 'The Soul of the Arabian Revolution', Asia, XX (April, May, June, July, August 1920), 259-66, 400-9, 517-25, 597-605, 670-6

——, 'Thomas Lawrence, Incognito', Asia, XXIV (November 1924), 854-8, 922-3

——, 'The Uncrowned King of Arabia', Strand, LIX (January, February, March, April 1920), 41-53, 141-53, 251-61, 330-8

——, 'War in the Land of the Arabian Nights', Asia, XIX (September, October, December 1919), 819-29, 998-1016, 1205-13

——, 'The White King of the Arabs', St. Nicholas, LIV (July, August, September, October 1927), 667-70, 746; 768-72, 840-1; 853-7, 937-8; 970-1, 1023-4

——, With Lawrence in Arabia, New York, 1924

B Thomas, Ronald, The Young Lawrence of Arabia, London, 1960

Thompson, Inspector Walter, Assignment: Churchill, New York, 1955. Pp. 8-41

Thurtle, Ernest, 'T.E. Lawrence', Time's Winged Chariot, London, 1945. Pp. 104-8

Tibawi, A.L., 'T.E. Lawrence, Feisal and Weizmann: The 1919 Attempt to Secure an Arab Balfour Declaration', Journal of the Royal Central Asian Society, LXI (1969), 156-163

'Lawrence Dead', Times /London7, 20 May 1935, p. 14

'Correspondence on the Extent of Lawrence's Arabic', TLS, 8, 15, 22, 29 June, 13, 20 July 1951, pp. 357, 373, 389, 405, 437, 454

Rev 'From Kinglake to Lawrence', TLS, 25 July 1935, pp. 468-70

Rev 'Lawrence and the Arabs', TLS, 10 March 1927, p. 151

Rev 'Lawrence of Arabia', TLS, 1 August 1935, p. 487

Rev 'Solitary Warrior', TLS, 1 June 1951, p. 340

Rev 'T.E. Lawrence in His Letters', TLS, 26 November 1938, p. 757

Rev 'To T.E. Lawrence', TLS, 19 June 1937, p. 460

Toynbee, Arnold, 'Colonel T.E. Lawrence', Acquaintances, London, 1967. Pp. 178-97

Tuchman, Barbara, Bible and Sword, New York, 1956. Pp. 204-10

Tudor, Harold, 'The Man Who Served With Lawrence in the Desert', Birmingham Evening Mail, 27 September 1962, p. 4

'Turkophil', 'The Colonel Lawrence Bogy', Near East and India, XXXV (14 February 1929), 205

Umari, Subhi al-, Lurans Kama Araftuh /Lawrence As I Have Known Him7, Beirut, 1969

* University of Texas: Humanities Research Center, T.E. Lawrence: Fifty Letters. 1920-1935. An Exhibition, Austin, 1962

Unstead, Robert, 'T.E.Lawrence', People in History, New York, 1957. Pp. 485-92

Van Der Meulen, D., The Wells of Ibn Saud, New York, 1957. Pp. 5, 10, 69-70, 74-5, 78-83, 257

Rev Van Doren, Mark, 'Lawrence of England', Nation, CXLI (6 November 1935), 545

Rev, R ——, 'Arabia Deserta' and 'Lawrence of England', The Private Reader, New York, 1942. Pp. 119-27, 216-18

Vansittart, Lord Robert, The Mist Procession: An Autobiography, London, 1968. Pp. 166, 205-6, 213-14, 234, 246, 260-1, 327, 365-6, 412

Vickery, Lt.-Col. C.E., 'Arabia and the Hedjaz', Journal of the Central Asian Society, X (1923), 46-67

* Villars, Jean Beraud, T.E. Lawrence, or The Search for the Absolute, New York, 1959

A.T.P.W., 'Lawrence in Oxford', Oxford Magazine, LIII (6 June 1935), 696-7

Wain, Noel, 'Crash that cost the world a hero and scarred a man for life', Evening Echo /Bournemouth7, 13 May 1966, p. 26

Walker, David, 'Lawrence of Arabia', Isis /Oxford7, 1504 (26 January 1966), 21

Walpole, Sir Hugh, 'T.E. Lawrence in Life and Death', Broadsheet (November 1939), n.p.

Warner, Oliver, 'Scott, Lawrence and the Myth of British Decadence', National Review, CXVII (September 1941), 314-17

Wavell, Archibald, Allenby: A Study in Greatness, New York, 1941

——, The Palestine Campaigns, London, 1929

F, R ——, 'T.E. Lawrence', The Good Soldier, London, 1948. Pp. 57-61

F, R ——, 'Unorthodox Soldiers: T.E. Lawrence', Soldiers and Soldiering, London, 1953. Pp. 95-100

* Weintraub, Stanley, 'Bernard Shaw's Other St. Joan', South Atlantic Quarterly, LXIV (Spring 1965), 194-205

——, 'How History Gets Rewritten: Lawrence of Arabia in the Theater', Drama Survey, II (1963), 269-75

Rev ——, 'Lawrence of Arabia', Film Quarterly (Spring 1964), p. 51

Rev ——, 'Legend Among the Bedouin', Saturday Review, XLVI (30 November 1963), 41

——, 'A Man Who Knew Lawrence of Arabia', Trenton Review, I (1966), 45-50

* ———, Private Shaw and Public Shaw, New York, 1963

Rev ———, 'The Secret Lives of Lawrence of Arabia', New York Times Book Review, 22 March 1970, pp. 8, 27

———, 'The Two Sides of "Lawrence of Arabia": Aubrey and Meek', Shaw Review, VII (May 1964), 54-7

Weizmann, Chaim, Trial and Error, New York, 1949. Pp. 234-5

Weller, Sam, 'Lawrence of Arabia and the Brough Superior', Cycle, XVIII (April 1967), 50-3, 74-5

Wemyss, Lady Wester, The Life and Letters of Lord Wester Wemyss. London, 1935. Pp. 275, 297, 336, 358-359, 410, 415

Rev West, Anthony, 'The Fascinator', New Yorker, XXXI (10 December 1955), 215-20

R ———, 'Miss Foster', David Rees, Among Others, New York, 1970

———, 'The Summer of the Hero', McCalls, XCVII (September 1970), 84-5, 103-4, 114-22

Rev, R ———, 'T.E. Lawrence', Principles and Persuasions: Literary Essays, London, 1958. Pp. 51-5

West, Herbert, The Mind on the Wing, New York, 1947. Pp. 88-93, 205-6

West, Rebecca and O'Toole, Peter, 'A Dialogue', Redbook, CXXII (March 1964), 56-7, 141, 146, 148-9

Wheeler, Keith, 'The Romantic Riddle of Lawrence of Arabia', Life, LII (12 January 1962), 94-108

Rev Wilkinson, Clennel, 'A Great Adventure', London Mercury, XVI (May 1927), 62-9

Rev Williams, Kenneth, 'Strange Self-Told Tales of T.E. Lawrence', Great Britain and the East, LI (1 December 1938), 597

Rev ———, 'T.E. Lawrence – Fact and Legend', Fortune, CXLIV (September 1935), 373-4

Williamson, Audrey, Bernard Shaw: Man and Writer, New York, 1963. Pp. 195-8

* Williamson, Henry, Genius of Friendship: T.E. Lawrence, London, 1941

———, The Gold Falcon, London, 1933

———, 'Threnos for T.E. Lawrence. I and II', The European, XV–XVI (May–June 1954), 44–61, 43–60

Wilson, Sir Arnold, Loyalties: Mesopotamia, London, 1936. I, 98, 161. II, 110, 194, 313, 320

Rev ———, 'Revolt in the Desert', Journal of the Central Asian Society, XIV (1927), 282–5

———, Thoughts and Talks, London, 1938. Pp. 33–5

Wilson, Colin, 'The Attempt to Gain Control', The Outsider, London: Pan, 1963. Pp. 75–90

———, Religion and the Rebel, Boston, 1957

Rev Winegarten, Renee, 'T.E. Lawrence: The End of a Legend', Mainstream, XVI (May 1970), 57–65

Wingate, Sir Ronald, Wingate of the Sudan, London, 1955. Pp. 188, 192–7

Winkler, Eugen, 'Obersten Lawrence', Gestalten und Probleme, Leipzig, 1937. Pp. 63–93

Winsten, Stephen, Days With Bernard Shaw, New York, 1949. Pp. 144, 176, 267–8

W. /Winterton, Lord Edward/, 'Arabian Nights and Days', Blackwood's Magazine, CCVII (May, June 1920), 585–608, 750–68

Winterton, Earl, Fifty Tumultuous Years, London, 1955. Pp. 64–73

Wirrek, E. /Pseud. of Fritz Steuben/, Emir Dynamit. Bilder aus dem Leben des Obersten Lawrence, Stuttgart, 1931

Rev Woodhouse, C.M., 'T.E. Lawrence: New Legends for Old', Twentieth Century, CLVII (March 1955), 228–36

Woodward, Ernest, Short Journey, London, 1942. Pp. 157–60

——— and Rohan Butler, eds. 'Policy of His Majesty's Government in Regard to Syria and Palestine, May 30, 1919–February 12, 1920'. Documents in British Foreign Policy, 1919–1939. 1st series, vol. IV, 1919. London: HMSO, 1952. Pp. 241–634

Rev Woolf, Leonard, 'The Epic of Modern Man', Nation and Atheneum, XL (19 March 1927), 857

Woolley, C. Leonard, As I Seem to Remember, London, 1962

——, 'Carchemish on the Euphrates', Spadework, London, 1953. Pp. 60-81

——, Dead Towns and Living Men, Oxford, 1929, pp. 101-77

R ——, 'Lawrence of Arabia as an Archeologist', The World of the Past, ed. Jacquetta Hawkes, New York, 1963. I, 117-18

Wrench, Sir Evelyn, Struggles, 1914-1920. London, 1935. Pp. 361-366, 419, 446, 449, 467

Wrench, John, 'Y.B. and T.E. Lawrence', Francis Yeats-Brown, 1886-1944, London, 1948. Pp. 130-44, 205, 228

Rev Yale, William, 'The Greatness of T.E. Lawrence', Yale Review, XXVIII (Summer 1939), 819-22

F Yeats-Brown, Francis, 'Lawrence As I Knew Him', Spectator, CLIV (24 May 1935), 872-3

R, F ——, 'Lawrence of Arabia as Critic and Friend', John O'London's Weekly, XXV (15 August 1936), 689-90

R, F ——, 'T.E. as Critic and Friend', Atlantic Monthly, CLVII (April 1936), 443-6

Young, Major Hubert, The Independent Arab, London, 1943

——, 'Makik: A Soldier in the Desert', Cornhill Magazine, LXI (October, November 1926), 409-28, 537-56

Zeine, Zeine, The Struggle for Arab Independence, Beirut, 1960

Zinsser, William, 'In Search of Lawrence of Arabia', Esquire, LV (June 1961), 101-4